PSYCHOANALYSIS

A FIRST BOOK

PSYCHOANALYSIS

FROM FREUD TO
THE AGE
OF THERAPY

EVE STWERTKA

FRANKLIN WATTS
NEW YORK • LONDON • TORONTO
SYDNEY • 1988

Photographs courtesy of: The Granger Collection: pp. 16, 21;
The Bettmann Archive, Inc.: pp. 24, 28, 35, 45, 57, 68; Brown
Brothers: pp. 26, 50, 74; Reuter/Bettmann Newsphotos: p. 38;
Springer/Bettmann Film Archive: p. 53; Mary Evans/Sigmund Freud
Copyrights: p. 71; Monkmeyer: p. 78 (Mimi Forsyth); Laimute E.
Druskis: p. 82; Photo Researchers, Inc.: p. 83 (Van Bucher).

Library of Congress Cataloging-in-Publication Data

Stwertka, Eve.
Psychoanalysis : from Freud to the age of therapy.

(A First book)
Bibliography: p.
Includes index.
Summary: Traces the development of psychoanalysis
through the work of Sigmund Freud and contrasts it with
more recent schools of psychotherapy.
1. Psychoanalysis—Juvenile literature. 2. Freud,
Sigmund, 1856–1939—Juvenile literature. 3. Psychoanalysts—Austria—Biography—Juvenile literature.
4. Psychotherapy—History—Juvenile literature.
[1. Psychoanalysis. 2. Freud, Sigmund, 1856–1939.
3. Psychotherapy] I. Title.
BF175.3.S79 1988.   150.19′5   87-7357
ISBN 0-531-10481-8

TO E. V.
NININGER, M.D.

CONTENTS

PSYCHOANALYSIS

INTRODUCTION

Sigmund Freud was a famous doctor who gave the world revolutionary new insights into human emotions and behavior. Now, you might think that a scientist who looks deep into people's minds could be a little forbidding and even scary. In reality, though, Dr. Freud was fair-minded, understanding, cheerful, and sociable. If you had visited him at home in Vienna, sometime around the early years of this century, you would probably have found him in his living room surrounded by a large family, a host of friends, and one or two visitors from abroad. If you had dropped in on him in the country during his summer vacation, he would certainly have asked you to join him on a hike in the Austrian mountains, along with his three girls and three boys.

Early photographs show Freud as a dark-eyed, handsome, intense young man. In later life, friends describe him as a companionable teller of jokes and stories. His interest in the history of civilization led him to a hobby of collecting the artwork of ancient cultures, such as Roman coins and Egyptian figurines.

Scientific inquiry was the highest kind of adventure for Freud. At the same time, though, helping people was central to his nature. Even in old age, when he was ill and in constant pain, he still wrote personal answers to strangers who asked him for advice. He was admirably courageous in confronting critics and enemies, and in enduring the hardships of war, illness, and exile. As a hard-working doctor, he went on treating patients almost until his death. As a thinker, he never stopped putting his ideas on paper. When his books and articles on psychology were published in a complete edition in 1959, they turned out, amazingly, to fill twenty-four volumes.

Although Freud influenced our thoughts on psychology forever, some of his controversial ideas continue to be debated, and some of the hardest questions he raised still remain to be answered.

I

A SCIENCE OF
THE MIND

The science concerned with the way people feel and think is called psychology. *Psyche* is a Greek word meaning "the soul" or "mind." According to an ancient Greek myth, Psyche was a beautiful girl who personified the soul. She was adored by Eros, the god of love. From the story we learn that when Eros and Psyche are joined together, they form the perfect union of body and mind that makes for a happy human being.

PSYCHOLOGICAL DISORDERS

Today psychology is divided into many branches of study. But in the late nineteenth century, when Sigmund Freud entered medical school at the University of Vienna, much less was known about the workings of the mind. Normal emotions such as love or fear were given little scientific consideration. They were mainly thought to be fit subjects for poets and philosophers. Only the most severe mental illnesses were of concern to doctors.

But many troubling disorders of the mind and soul lie between these two extremes. These disorders can make people miserable, spoil their lives, and even incapacitate them. They include symptoms such as depression and anxiety without apparent reason, pains and disabilities without physical cause, fears that seem unfounded and exaggerated, and other mental and emotional torments. Doctors before Freud's time often overlooked and disregarded these problems because there was little they could do to relieve them. It was Freud who first discovered that these symptoms were the outward signs of hidden inner processes which could be studied and explored by new methods.

At the leading German medical schools of that time, the most modern professors believed that whatever happens in a living organism must be explainable by the laws of chemistry and physics. Therefore any trouble of the mind could only be caused by trouble in the body. Even a psychological illness must spring from a physical cause. Emotional problems were called "nervous disorders," or *neuroses*, because they were thought to result from some fault in the patient's nervous system.

As a young *neurologist* (a doctor specializing in the structure and diseases of the nervous system), Sigmund Freud tried to discover exactly how and where the mind and the body interact. But he had no success, and he gave up his attempt to find a physical approach to emotional disorders. Even though Freud never abandoned the systematic thinking of the biologist, he struck out for an entirely new approach to the riddles of the human psyche. To find out what ailed the people who came to him for help, Freud analyzed their actions, words, and dreams. He also looked closely at himself, his friends, and his family. He even examined folktales, literature, myths, and religions. No human urge escaped his inquiry. From these investigations, which became his life's work, he developed the method of treatment he named *psychoanalysis*. This term also describes the system of ideas about the human mind that was developed by Freud, his associates, and his successors.

BEGINNINGS

Sigmund Freud was born on May 6, 1856, in a part of Austria that now belongs to Czechoslovakia. Even then, the little wooded country town of his birth had two names. It was called Freiberg in German and Pribor in Czech. Both the German and Czech languages were spoken by the townspeople, which was only the first of several puzzling circumstances that Sigmund had to mull over in his young mind.

Freud's father had been married once before, but his first wife had died and left him with two grown sons. The older of these, who lived nearby, already had a boy of his own and was soon to have a little girl. This presented another interesting puzzle for Sigmund: he was born an uncle.

Freud's mother was very young, pretty, and cheerful. Sigmund had the privileged position of being her firstborn child. After him, though, in rather quick succession, came five girls and two more boys. Freud's father, Jakob, owned a small textile business, but it could not provide for such a large family. Before long, the family was forced to move to Vienna, the Austrian capital.

Yet another puzzling situation impressed Sigmund early in life. On Sundays and holidays, bells rang out from a high tower with a pointed steeple, calling the people of Pribor to church. Just about everyone for miles around was Roman Catholic. The Freud family, however, was Jewish, which made them part of a very small minority.

The Jews of Austria had been legally emancipated only eight years before Freud's birth. Sigmund never forgot a story his father told him. Once, as a young fellow, Jakob Freud was walking down the street when a man coming the other way knocked off his cap and pushed him from the sidewalk, shouting, "Out of my way, Jew!"

"What did you do about it?" the boy wanted to know. But Jakob merely shrugged. He had picked up his cap and walked on.

Sigmund would have preferred to have his father take a more heroic role. Later, when Sigmund learned history in school, he chose a very different hero for himself. It was Hannibal, the great general of ancient Carthage who crossed the Alps into Italy and several times attacked and defeated his archenemies, the mighty Romans.

The Freud family, about 1876.
Sigmund is standing, third from left.
His mother, Amalie, is sitting in
front of Sigmund, and his father,
Jakob, is to her left.

When the time came for him to choose a career, Freud found himself wishing he, too, could be a great military leader or statesman. But in Austria, at that time, such careers were closed to young men of Jewish families. Business, law, or medicine were the most likely alternatives, and Freud ended up choosing the latter.

An idea that we have learned from Freud's writing is that a child's early experiences help determine the kind of person he or she will eventually become. If we look at Freud himself, we can see some of the forces that helped shape the future man. He identified with Hannibal, the victorious soldier, but the land he set out to conquer was the unknown territory of the human mind.

2

HYSTERIA AND HYPNOSIS

Imagine the labor of dissecting four hundred eels and examining them under a microscope! This was one of Freud's first projects as a university student. Next, as a research assistant at the Vienna Physiological Institute, he went to work investigating the microscopic structure of nerve cells in fish. The instruments he used were primitive, and the job took endless patience. But to him it was an adventure into the unknown instead of a chore.

During his years of graduate study, Freud contributed to knowledge about evolution and made some important discoveries about nerve cells. He also anticipated the use of cocaine as a local anesthetic, and felt pleased when, not long afterward, it enabled his own father to be one of the first patients to undergo a painless eye operation.

MEDICAL STUDIES

Freud would have liked to go on working in the laboratory, if only he could have made a living at it. Unfortunately, research was paid only by small grants and fellowships. His father was elderly and had stopped earning an income some time ago, and his mother and sisters were living in poverty. The only sensible solution for him was to become a doctor, specializing in neurology. In 1881 he received the grade "excellent" on his final medical examinations.

To gain clinical experience Freud spent three years as a resident in Vienna's General Hospital. At the Psychiatric Clinic he worked long, hard hours observing mentally ill patients. He read intensively, attended lectures, and became deeply absorbed in brain anatomy. His special field of interest was the medulla oblongata, the part of the brain that lies at the back of the head and is continuous with the spinal cord.

Freud was a brilliant student, surrounded by first-rate minds. At the same time, though, he was struck by how little psychiatrists seemed to understand about their subject and their patients. Psychiatric treatments often consisted of nothing more than hot and cold showers or applications of electric current. Patients who were well enough to stay out of an institution were prescribed rest or exercise, ocean bathing or mountain air—provided that they could afford these luxuries.

THE CASE OF ANNA O.

One Viennese doctor, though, Joseph Breuer (1842–1925), was experimenting with an entirely new and different treatment method. Freud was fascinated by his friend Breuer's account of a patient he called "Miss Anna O." Miss O., whose real name was Bertha Pappenheim, had long suffered from several different emotional and

The famous "Anna O.," later revealed to be Bertha Pappenheim, was treated by Joseph Breuer for hysteria. Breuer's therapeutic treatment of Anna O. aroused Freud's interest in this kind of disorder.

physical symptoms, all belonging to the puzzling group of disorders called *hysteria*.

Breuer's treatment sessions consisted simply of allowing her to "talk away" her symptoms by tracing their history back to the events she associated with them in her memory. He called his technique the cathartic method (from the Greek word *catharsis*, meaning "cleansing"). Miss O. used to refer to these mind-cleansing sessions as "chimney sweeping."

But the patient's long, concentrated bouts of talking about herself took so much of the doctor's time and energy that Breuer was not anxious to try the method on anyone else. He and Freud discussed the meaning of this strange case endlessly. But for the moment they could only speculate whether or not the treatment was valid in a general way.

DR. CHARCOT'S CLINIC

Freud was now officially a doctor of neuropathology, and getting ready to publish some of his important research on the anatomy of the brain. He was invited to take charge of the neurological department in a private clinic for children. He later became a leading authority on infantile cerebral paralysis.

Meanwhile, though, he was aware that symptoms of paralysis often appeared in cases of hysteria, and Breuer's work with Anna O. had aroused his interest in this group of disorders. In Paris, a famous doctor, Jean Martin Charcot (1825–1893), was having amazing success treating hysteria by means of *hypnosis*. Neurologists from all over the world were drawn to Charcot's hospital. They marveled at the wealth of interesting cases and studied the great medical man's unusual methods. Freud entered a tough competition for a government travel grant and won a fellowship to work six months under Charcot in Paris.

The timing was perfect. Freud had recently become engaged, was deeply in love, and could hardly wait to earn a secure enough income so he could get married. Half-joking, he wrote to his fiancée, Martha Bernays, "I shall go to Paris and become a great savant (scientist) and return to Vienna with a great, great nimbus (halo of success). Then we will marry soon and I will cure all the incurable nervous patients and . . . (we will live) happily ever after."

THE POWER
OF SUGGESTION

The disorder called hysteria took many different forms. Some patients came to Charcot's clinic because they were unable to move a leg or an arm, or had no feeling in some part of the body. Others came because they could not eat or felt unexplained pains. Of course, these symptoms could have been caused by injury, stroke, or brain tumor. But if all such physical causes were ruled out by medical examination, the patient was diagnosed a "hysteric."

The name *hysteria* was taken from the Greek word for the womb. In earlier times, when not much was known about the human body, there was a theory that the womb sometimes became detached from its proper place in a woman's abdomen and wandered about unpredictably, causing all kinds of damage that could not be accounted for otherwise. Although by Freud's day this superstition had long been laid to rest, doctors still didn't understand hysteria much better than their predecessors. The name had stuck and the disorder was still considered typical for women rather than for men.

Charcot's procedure with hysterical patients was to place them under hypnosis. This is a relaxed and sleeplike state, in which the patient loses awareness of the surroundings but can still hear and speak with the doctor. For reasons unknown even today, people under hypnosis respond obediently to suggestions made by the hypnotist. After awakening, they have no memory of the hypnotic session. And yet, if the hypnotist has given them any task to carry out, they will immediately perform it, without seeming to know why.

Dr. Charcot used this power of the hypnotist in his clinical prac-

tice. Having placed his patients under hypnosis, he would talk to them about their condition and would end by telling them that their particular symptom was passing off and would be cured by the time they woke up. In an amazing number of cases this was, indeed, what happened.

Even more surprisingly, Charcot showed that the opposite effect could also be achieved. A healthy person under hypnosis could be induced to experience hysterical symptoms and to show real signs of pain or distress. For example, the hypnotist might suggest to a man under hypnosis, "Your right leg is turning quite stiff; you are not able to bend your knee." Sure enough, the man would start limping stiff-legged across the room. Even after he emerged from the hypnotic state, the stiffness in the knee would remain for a while longer.

Whereas Charcot and others held on to the conviction that hysteria must be caused by some inherited organic weakness, young Freud—mindful of Breuer's success with Anna O.—suspected that its origins were psychological. At the same time, he recognized that there was nothing faked or imaginary about its symptoms. The physical and mental suffering of patients was entirely real. Further, he saw many male patients who were brought to Charcot's clinic and realized that hysteria, far from being peculiar to women, was a universal phenomenon.

What Freud witnessed in Paris went against the grain of his previous medical training. He had been taught to believe that psychic disorders must be related to some physical cause. How was it possible, then, for an illness to come or go in response to an idea?

Sigmund Freud and his fiancée,
Martha Bernays, in Berlin in 1885,
the year before their marriage

A TURNING POINT

The young neurologist went back to Vienna in 1886, deep in thought and eager to begin the hypnotic treatment of hysterical patients in his own practice.

For some years longer, he continued his attempt to pinpoint just how and where brain, mind, nerves, and *psyche* meet and act on each other. More than once he wrote to Wilhelm Fliess (1858–1928), a German doctor who was his best friend and favorite correspondent at that time, that he was laboring over a "psychology for neurologists." The outcome of these efforts was his *Project for a Scientific Psychology*, which Freud finally finished in 1895. He had set out "to see how the theory of mental functioning takes shape if quantitative considerations, a sort of economics of nerveforce, are introduced into it. . . ."

But in Freud's own eyes, the "Project" was a failure. He set it aside and from that time on stopped speculating about the anatomical seat of the emotions. He was resigned to speaking about "regions in the mental apparatus, wherever they may be situated in the body." And so, after being a neurologist, he became a psychoanalyst.

In one of her reminiscences, Anna Freud, Sigmund's famous daughter, describes a picture that hung in her father's study in Vienna. It showed a hospital scene of a doctor demonstrating something to a group of students. Their gaze is directed at a patient, a

Jean Martin Charcot, the French physician who pioneered in the use of hypnosis in treating hysterical patients. The six months Freud spent working under Charcot were to have a profound influence on him.

*In the painting that hung in Freud's
study in Vienna, Dr. Charcot is shown
giving a dramatic demonstration to
students in his famous clinic.*

young woman in a half-fainting state, whose slender waist is being supported by an attendant.

"What's wrong with that lady?" Anna often asked. Her father would always answer that the lady was suffering from wearing her corset too tightly laced—a frequent problem in those days of the fashionable wasp waist. But Anna could tell from his thoughtful smile that the picture had a special meaning for him.

In fact, the picture was a scene from Professor Charcot's clinic, a souvenir Freud had brought home with him from Paris. His half-year of study there had proved a memorable turning point in his life and career.

THE TALKING CURE

In big cities there are bound to be many people with emotional problems, and Vienna was no exception. Patients came flocking to Sigmund Freud. One such patient was a young married woman who wanted to breast-feed her first baby but was prevented from doing so by fits of vomiting and a lack of milk. To her grief, the baby had to be sent away, to be fed by a wet nurse. When she gave birth to her second child the same thing happened. This time, though, she underwent two hypnotic sessions with Freud, which cured her completely and enabled her to nurse the baby for eight months. After the birth of her third child, her disability returned once more. Again, hypnosis with Freud made it possible for her to nurse the baby with her own milk.

A NEW APPROACH

This kind of success raised Freud's reputation with the public but earned him disapproval from the German medical community. He was accused of abandoning science and playing with magic. Some former colleagues came close to calling him a faker.

Freud himself was not entirely pleased with what he was doing. Often, he was unable to induce a hypnotic state deep enough for a treatment to work. Even when it did work, many symptoms had a way of coming back later, when the patient was no longer under his influence. Not only that. Freud soon came to dislike the hypnotic relationship because of the way he constantly had to assert his own will over the will of those who came to him for help.

Reflecting on Joseph Breuer's experiences with Anna O., Freud began to suspect that hypnosis might not be a necessary step in treating neurotic patients at all. Following his senior colleague's lead, he tried omitting hypnosis and simply encouraged his patients to ease their minds by talking.

Sure enough, when people spoke freely in the privacy of the doctor's office, not only their current problems but also long-forgotten experiences, fears, and fantasies would rise from the depths of memory to the surface of their minds. Freud soon surmised that these must be connected to the patient's present illness, because bringing them out into the open often had the mysterious effect of relieving the symptoms. One grateful patient dubbed this treatment "the talking cure."

THE CASE OF
FRAU CECILY M.

Sometime in 1887, Joseph Breuer called in Freud to treat a wealthy, aristocratic woman who suffered from hysteria, depression, anxiety, headaches, and other illnesses. "Frau (Mrs.) Cecily M." as Freud later referred to her in his writings, was intelligent, lively, and imaginative. She was the mother of five children, wrote poetry, and played chess well enough to keep two games going at once. But in spite of all her accomplishments, she was plagued by mental and physical anguish.

In those days doctors still made house calls, and twice daily, when Frau M. suffered a crisis, Freud was summoned to her mansion. Since her illness forced her to spend most of her time lying on a lounge chair in her room, this is where her treatment sessions took place. Evidently Freud found the use of the couch practical because he soon placed one in his office for patients to lie on when they came to see him there.

In later years Freud spoke about "Frau Cecily M." as his teacher. Visiting her twice daily for three years, observing her symptoms, listening to her thoughts, and tracing her cries and groans to their connection with her reminiscences, gave him a unique education in the workings of a hysterical patient's mind.

Unfortunately, he did not succeed in curing this memorable teacher of his. Even before he began her treatment she had become addicted to the drug morphine. As her drug dependence increased, her state of mind worsened, making analysis impossible. How she and Freud parted is not known because her wealth and social position helped to keep a veil of privacy over her illness. In fact, her real identity has only recently been established, by the scholar Peter J. Swales. He discusses it in his essay "Freud, His Teacher and the Birth of Psychoanalysis."

THE UNCONSCIOUS

What the two doctors observed confirmed what Freud had begun to suspect in Dr. Charcot's clinic. The human psyche was more profound than medical science had ever reckoned. Under the surface of our awareness there must be a deeper layer. This inner mind, of which we have no inkling, has, as it were, a life of its own. Without asking our intellect for permission, it can influence our feelings and our behavior. And even though we are not in touch with it, it is nevertheless real, powerful, and always with us. Eventually, Freud coined the term *the unconscious* for this secret part of the self.

TRAUMATIC EXPERIENCES

In medical language, a violent shock to some part of the body is called a trauma. Working together, Freud and Breuer discovered that an experience of fright, shame, or pain could act as a trauma on the emotions, and thus form the starting point of hysterical symptoms.

Freud surmised that when the mind wants to get rid of extremely distressing experiences, it buries them in the unconscious, hoping that they will lie there and remain "forgotten." Unfortunately, though, being hidden from the wear and tear of daily life, they remain forever fresh. And as new events come into people's lives and threaten to revive the buried trauma, a whole network of reactions may be built up to keep the trauma from becoming conscious. Freud called the process of pushing things into the unconscious part of the mind *repression*. The devices that people use to aid them in keeping repressed ideas from becoming conscious, he called *defenses*. It was the effort involved in repression and defense that engendered the hysterical symptoms.

To treat psychological symptoms, Freud asked his patients to retrace a path in their minds, back to the source of their illness, as if they were following a thread through the labyrinth of memory. Eventually, they would reach the root itself, with all its distressful feelings still attached. In an early report on his and Breuer's work, Freud wrote, "each individual hysterical symptom immediately and permanently disappeared when we had succeeded in bringing clearly to light the memory of the event by which it was provoked." It is important to keep in mind, though, that relief only came after the patient had *worked through* the traumatic experience and suffered once more the strong emotions that forced him or her to repress it in the first place.

DEFENSE MECHANISMS

Unlike hysteria, which bypasses the emotions and takes the form of physical symptoms, many psychic disorders express themselves

Sigmund Freud at age thirty-five

mainly in mental states such as depression and anxiety. Still others appear as *phobias* or fears. People who are phobic may suffer acutely in crowds or in tunnels, crossing bridges, or standing in wide open places, or at the thought of being attacked by people or by dogs. Such phobias can become strong enough to prevent a patient from leaving his or her house.

Neurosis may also be expressed in compulsive acts such as constant hand washing or endless checking to see if one has locked the door. Freud marveled at the great profusion and variety in which such symptoms could occur. Basically, though, he considered them all ways to avoid becoming conscious of repressed thoughts. In other words, the symptoms of neurosis are *defense mechanisms*.

THE PLEASURE PRINCIPLE

To make sense of what was happening in the talking cure, Freud worked out a tentative scheme that he continued to elaborate until the end of his life. It rested on the idea that for best survival the psychic system needs to maintain a constant equilibrium. Stimulation reaches the system from outside, as well as from inside itself. Excessive stimulation is painful because it upsets the equilibrium, and the reduction of stimulation is pleasurable because it restores the balance. And so, to avoid the disturbing excitement of an unpleasant idea, the mind seeks to get rid of it by burying it in the unconscious. Repression and resistance, then, are based on the *pleasure principle*.

ON THE COUCH

Even today, the item of furniture essential to an analyst's office is the famous psychoanalytic couch. Freud's first use of the couch was probably in the home of his patient "Frau Cecily M." Later, he used it in his office in Vienna, to help people relax and approach a sleeplike state without having to be hypnotized. He would ask his patients to lie down, while he sat on a chair behind them. Freud did not want them to be distracted by his presence or his facial expressions. He encouraged patients to close their eyes and concentrate on a particular symptom, trying to recall everything that might reveal its origin. He particularly impressed on his patients that they must not censor anything that came to mind, even if it seemed embarrassing, unpleasant, or just plain boring to them. By listening closely, Freud could then trace the patient's unconscious thought patterns.

Because this process leaves the mind at liberty to roam without direction or censorship, Freud named it *free association*. Even today it remains part of the basic technique of psychoanalysis.

THE TRANSFERENCE

To Freud's surprise, patients in treatment very often declared strong feelings of love for him. One woman even threw her arms around his neck, and only the entrance of a servant saved doctor and patient from further embarrassment. Since he was a stranger to his patients and gave them no encouragement to love him, Freud soon realized that so many people couldn't possibly be enamored of his real self. Their feelings had actually been formed long ago and were originally directed toward their parents or others on whom they had been dependent. The treatment situation, in which the doctor seemed to play the role of a father and the patient the role of a child, was responsible for this *transference*. Love was not the only emotion a patient might transfer to him. There were others, such as anger, suspicion, jealousy, and fear.

Eventually, Freud recognized the transference as a necessary stage in psychoanalysis. It enables patient and doctor to understand the unconscious memories and feelings simmering under the surface. By repeating and wrestling with childhood relationships, the patient works free of them.

In talking about the transference with his colleagues, Freud

came to realize that there is also such a thing as a *countertransference*. After all, analysts are human, too, and can't help responding to the people they treat with emotions of their own. But the treatment would end in total confusion if the doctor's feelings toward the patient went beyond professional interest and sympathy. To keep the analyst's insights free from emotional interference, Freud insisted that before they could treat others, analysts must undergo a training analysis of their own. This has continued to be a requirement to this day.

THE SEDUCTION THEORY

A strange but definite pattern emerged from the stories that people told during the talking cure. When they let their minds roam freely, the patients would often recall an early sexual experience of some kind, sometimes going back even to the first few years of their childhood.

Bear in mind that social relations in nineteenth-century Vienna were strict and proper. Sex was not mentioned among ladies and gentlemen, and every effort was made to keep young people in ignorance of it until just before marriage. As for children, sexual feelings were assumed to be simply nonexistent in their lives. Therefore it came as a surprise to Freud that so many patients recalled sexual memories from childhood. Even more serious was that these

Early in his career, Freud hit upon the idea of using a couch for his patients to lie on as they underwent psychoanalysis. The couch in this photograph is the one he used when he lived in London after 1938.

memories often involved the parent of the opposite sex, or else some uncle, nursemaid, or family friend. The regular recurrence of such memories in his patients led Freud to formulate one of his most important principles, namely that neuroses derive their fundamental origin from the repression of sexual traumas in childhood.

At first, Freud believed, however reluctantly, that an enormous amount of child seduction and child abuse was practiced in the middle-class homes from which his patients mostly came. Later, though, the frequency with which patients reported having been seduced by a parent or guardian caused Freud serious doubts. By 1897 he had come to think that most patients' tales of early seduction were fantasies rather than facts.

Recently, critics have blamed Freud for steering away from his *seduction theory*. They believe he was unwilling to face the terrible reality of child abuse in his patients' early lives. Whatever the truth may be, his change of mind did not greatly alter the nature of psychoanalytic treatment. After all, Freud never claimed that it was the traumatic experience itself that caused the patient psychological harm, but rather the repression of the trauma. The unconscious is not very good at distinguishing fact from fiction, and a repressed traumatic fantasy could be as damaging as a repressed memory. Both fantasy and reality were always relevant to Freud. Finding out the exact truth of a patient's past is not the important thing in psychoanalysis. Rather, it is how unconscious factors in the mind affect the way the patient copes with his or her present life.

CHAPTER

DREAMS

Often, while letting their minds roam from thought to thought in the process called *free association*, the people who came to Freud's couch would tell him their dreams. Because dreams arise during sleep, a time when the conscious mind is not in control, Freud eventually became convinced that dreams are "the royal road to the unconscious." In fact, he soon realized that this was a universal principle, true as much for the dreams of healthy persons as for those of his patients.

Freud himself was a sound sleeper and prolific dreamer. Observing how his dreams tied in to his waking life, he was struck by some brilliant new ideas about the function of dreaming. In 1900 he published these ideas in *The Interpretation of Dreams*, the book that contributed most to making him famous. Even to the end of his life, it remained Freud's favorite among his own books.

WISHES IN DISGUISE

We tend to speak about a very special wish as a "dream," and our so-called daydreams are usually filled with wishful thinking. It occurred to Freud that the dreams we have while we sleep must be wishes too, but mostly wishes in disguise.

In the simplest kind of dream the wish is quite obvious. Freud reports how he once overheard one of his children talk in her sleep about strawberries and hot cereal. Evidently she was very hungry, for, having had an upset stomach the day before, she had been put to bed without supper. Her dream about food, then, was a simple wish fulfillment.

Another common kind of dream arises when some outside noise, such as an alarm clock, threatens to wake us up. This is illustrated by Freud's story of a medical student who received a wake-up call to report for duty at the hospital. Being exhausted, the young doctor slept on. While he slept, he dreamed that he looked at a chart over a hospital bed and noticed that it had his own name on it. As Freud points out, the man seemed to be telling himself, "I'm already in the hospital, so I don't have to wake up and go there." The disguised wish, in this case, was simply the wish to continue sleeping.

Ultimately, Freud came to think that all dreams occur in response to some stimulus which threatens to disturb sleep. The purpose of dreaming is to preserve the sleeper's psychic balance so that he or she will not have to wake up. This makes every dream "the guardian of sleep," as Freud put it.

The stimulus that provokes a dream to form might be external to the sleeper. It might be a noise, a touch, a feeling of heat or cold. More often, the stimulus is likely to be internal. Hunger, thirst, pain, even the need to urinate, all threaten to disrupt sleep. The dreams provoked by such bodily sensations tend to make us feel that the momentary need is taken care of, so that we won't need to awaken.

Many other factors contribute to the forming of a dream. Events of the previous day, conflicts, unsolved problems, childhood memories, all have a part. In a beautiful image, Freud compares the growth of a dream to the way a mushroom forms in the woods, out of a mysterious tangle of underground filaments.

DISTORTIONS

But why do so many dreams seem foolish or grotesque? According to Freud, the most frequent stimulus for a dream is some disturbing thought that enters the mind and endangers the sleeper's rest. The psychic system defends itself by distorting the dream content or by dressing it in disguise so that the sleeping consciousness is not disturbed.

To be sure, the censorship the human mind practices on itself is reduced during sleep. But even so, a dream can be compared to a censored letter. To get the letter past the censor, the person writing it has to use hints and roundabout expressions, leave out certain parts, and sometimes say the opposite of what is meant. It takes inside information to understand the message. Because dreams often fulfill conflicted, repressed, disguised childhood wishes, they are likely to appear weird, disconnected, vague, or illogical.

COMPOSITES AND SUBSTITUTES

The unconscious works much like the imagination. To make dreams, it uses the same devices that go into making myths, fairy tales, and literature. Take a lizard's shape, for instance, combine it with the size and fierceness of a bear, and you have a dragon. In dreams we create similar composites that have a logic of their own.

Let's look at an example. Freud once dreamed that his friend R. was his uncle. In the dream R.'s face looked a little changed and elongated and was surrounded with a yellow beard.

When Freud remembered this dream in the morning, his first reaction was to laugh out loud and call it nonsense. But he reminded himself that when his patients called a dream nonsense it was usually a sign of strong resistance to interpretation. Some disagreeable thought was likely to be hidden under the nonsensical disguise. Thereupon, Freud forced himself to analyze his dream by free association.

Although he had five uncles, his first thought on examining the dream was of his Uncle Joseph. This uncle, unfortunately, had once acted dishonestly and had been punished by the authorities. At the time, Freud's father, whose hair was said to have turned gray as a result of this disgrace, gently excused this brother by speaking of him as "a simpleton."

Many dreams substitute one person for another, so as to hide the true identity of the one the dream is really about. In this particular dream, Freud's friend R. had a long face and a yellow beard. But in reality he was very dark haired, though turning gray, like Freud himself. The blond beard and long face belonged to Uncle Joseph as a young man. The dreamer had created a composite by combining two people into one. This device of identification seemed to state: "R. is just like Uncle Joseph, so he must be a dishonest simpleton."

But why, Freud asks himself, should he dream such an insult to his highly respected and educated friend? Thinking further, Freud remembers that both he and R. are candidates for a professorship at the university. Both men were Jewish. Will this hurt their chances? In private conversation, both admitted worrying that religious considerations might influence the committee in charge of the appointments. In that case, even their high professional standing would not be enough to make them acceptable.

The dream, then, gives Freud the following reassurance: "If R. doesn't get the university professorship it's because he is a dishonest simpleton. Religious considerations have played no part in his rejection, and so my own chances remain good."

DREAM SYMBOLS

Dreams speak in symbols. A symbol is basically a comparison. The human body, for instance, can be compared to a house, the eyes

A caricature of Freud analyzing a figure of himself lying on a couch, spouting Freudian imagery

to windows, the inner organs to rooms and corridors. The mind has a natural capacity for this kind of comparing and substituting, and even very small children are adept at it. The dreaming mind also likes to express ideas as pictures. In a dream about someone "in a high position," for example, you might literally see this person placed in an elevated spot such as a speaker's platform or a stage.

Although most dream symbols are personal and unique, Freud does recognize some that are universal. In fact, these are already familiar to us through literature and folklore. King and queen tend to stand for father and mother, prince and princess for son and daughter. Children tend to be represented by small animals. But depending on the dream's hidden mood children might appear as cute puppies or, at the other extreme, as horrifying beetles.

Freud first drew attention to the common occurrence of sexual symbolism in dreams. Since sex is both central to life and very private, it is subject to a great deal of repression. Childhood curiosity, adolescent exploration, and adult activity are all kept hidden to some extent and have a tendency to emerge in the unconscious in symbolic form. Freud found that in dreams the male sex organ may be represented by all sorts of long, pointed objects, such as sticks, tree trunks, knives, guns, or umbrellas. The female organ tends to be represented by boxes, ovens, ships, rooms, and other cavities and containers.

The open way Freud spoke about these and other sexual symbols often provoked a mixture of outrage and mockery. He was accused of overstressing the sexual elements in the human psyche. In *The Interpretation of Dreams* Freud takes up these objections. He explains that it is not surprising if the majority of the dreams of adults deal with sexual material. "No other instinct has had to undergo so much suppression, from the time of childhood onwards . . . from no other instinct are so many and such intense unconscious wishes left over, which now, in the sleeping state, generate dreams." But, he continues, "the assertion that 'all dreams call for a sexual interpretation,' . . . is quite foreign to my 'Interpretation of Dreams.' It will not be found in any of the eight editions of this book. . . ."

THE DREAM OF
THE BURNING CHILD

Some dreams seem mystical or prophetic. Freud cites such a dream and shows that here, too, the laws of unconscious *wish fulfillment* are at work. Here is his account in *The Interpretation of Dreams*.

> A father had been watching day and night beside the sick-bed of his child. After the child died, he retired to rest in an adjoining room but left the door ajar so that he could look from his room into the next, where the child's body lay surrounded by tall candles. An old man, who had been installed as a watcher, sat beside the body, murmuring prayers. After sleeping for a few hours the father dreamed that the child was standing by his bed, clasping his arm and crying reproachfully: "Father, don't you see that I am burning?" The father woke up and noticed a bright light coming from the adjoining room. Rushing in, he found that the old man had fallen asleep, and the sheets and one arm of the beloved body were burnt by a fallen candle.

Freud thought this frightening dream was quite simple to interpret. The external stimulus for the dream was the sudden blaze of bright light from the half-open door, which correctly made the father think of fire. At the same time, the words "don't you see that I am burning" recall the child's high fever before dying. The wish fulfillment in the dream is twofold. Foremost in the father's mind is the wish that the child were still alive. In the dream, this is granted when the living child touches his arm and speaks. The second wish is to remain asleep a little longer, for in remaining asleep and dreaming, he keeps the child by his side.

Although the father's sleep was disturbed by the light, the thought that the child's body might have caught fire did not immediately wake him. Instead, the dream allowed him to prolong the child's presence for one moment longer. In Freud's view, even a nightmare serves as a wish fulfillment in its own strange way.

THE RIDDLE OF THE SPHINX

As a young, ambitious medical student, Freud used to imagine that one day his portrait would be carved in stone and put up in the courtyard of the University of Vienna like those of the famous professors of the past. The inscription he had in mind for himself came from the ancient Greek play about King Oedipus: "Who guessed the famous riddle and was a man most mighty."

Strangely enough, on his fiftieth birthday a group of Freud's supporters presented him with a medal showing Oedipus confronting the monster called the Sphinx. Freud turned pale on reading the inscription. It was exactly the one he had picked for himself in his secret, youthful fantasy.

THE STORY OF OEDIPUS

There are many reasons why Freud was fascinated by this ancient myth. Oedipus was a great discoverer who suffered an ironic fate. At his birth it was predicted that he would kill his father and marry his mother. And though he went out of his way to avoid it, he ended up killing a man and marrying a woman who—as he learned too late—were his parents after all. To punish himself for not seeing things clearly, he put out his eyes and went into exile as a blind beggar.

In spite of this doom, Oedipus has always been regarded as a hero because he was a bold seeker after the truth. His first heroic act was to defeat the Sphinx. This creature, part woman, part lion, and part bird, ravaged the city of Thebes and devoured people who could not answer her riddle. The question she asked was, "What goes on four legs in the morning, two legs at noon, and three legs at night?" Oedipus answered, "It's a human being. As babies we crawl on all fours, as adults we walk upright on two legs, and in old age we hobble on three legs, one of which is a cane."

The Sphinx killed herself in a rage at having her secret found out, and Oedipus was made king of Thebes. The widowed queen, whose former husband was said to have been murdered while traveling, became Oedipus's wife. Afterwards, plague struck the city and it became necessary to find the killer of the former king. Oedipus again boldly sought the truth. To his grief he discovered that he himself was the killer, that the king had been his father, that the queen was not only his wife but also his mother, and that his own presence was the cause of the plague.

THE OEDIPUS COMPLEX

Oedipus learned that although he could not change his fate, he did have the power to search and inquire. Freud, too, was forever in pursuit of truth, and like Oedipus, he asked the question, "Who am I?"

Around the age of forty, at a time when his life seemed to be going very well, Sigmund Freud had begun to suffer from depres-

According to Greek myth, when Oedipus answered the riddle of the Sphinx, the Sphinx, in a rage, killed herself, and Oedipus was crowned king of Thebes.

sion, fatigue, and migraine headaches. In the summer of 1897, he decided to find the cause of his problems and embarked on an inward journey to psychoanalyze his own unconscious.

Jakob Freud, his father, had died the previous autumn and, as Sigmund wrote to a friend, ". . . inside me the occasion of his death has reawakened all my early feelings. Now I feel quite uprooted." His mother was still alive, however, and he continued to enjoy the sense of being her favorite and most successful son. Surrounded by a flock of his own six young children, he was able to experience at first hand the joys and tensions of the unique relationship he later named "the family romance."

All of these circumstances contributed to the formation of Freud's central theory of human development, the *Oedipus complex*. In his book on dreams that he was writing at about the same time, he notes that it is not uncommon for men to dream about having sexual relations with their mothers. Even more common, however, are dreams that enact the story of Oedipus under various disguises. Elements such as the father's death or disappearance, the mother's favor, and some kind of punishment or mutilation occurred repeatedly in his patients' dreams as well as in his own. He also observed that the children within a family (the siblings, as social scientists call them) compete with one another for the favor of their parents. *Sibling rivalry* is particularly intense in vying for the love of the parent of the opposite sex.

From these observations Freud deduced that on the way to growing up, every small boy goes through a stage of being in love with his mother, wishing to marry her, and wishing all his rivals— especially his father—out of the way. In a child's limited understanding, this means wishing they were dead.

As a result of these Oedipal wishes, the boy feels guilty and becomes afraid that his all-powerful father will deal him a terrible punishment. In the Oedipus myth the hero punishes himself by removing his eyes. Freud believed that the eyes, in this case, were a symbolic substitute for an equally precious body part—the male

In this theatrical version of Sophocles's Oedipus Rex, *Oedipus is shown being hailed by the citizens of Thebes.*

sex organ. A boy in the Oedipal stage unconsciously fears that his father will take revenge by injuring the boy's penis or even castrating him. This fear, however, will eventually make the boy give up his desire for his mother and turn toward other goals. When this happens, the boy is successfully on the way to becoming a healthy adult. If, however, this does not happen at the proper time, the demands of adult life are likely to precipitate the young man into a neurotic crisis.

Freud saw the development of young women as a parallel process (called the Electra complex). The little girl is enamored of her father, wishes to have a baby with him, resents and fears her mother, but finally transfers her affection from her father to her husband. If she is unable to do so, she will be plunged into the kind of conflict that engenders neurosis.

It is easy to imagine that many doctors and psychiatrists rejected the theory of the Oedipus complex with distaste, ridicule, or stony silence. Whereas Freud took pride in having divined a deeply significant riddle, others accused him of obscenity. At the same time, though, he attracted a group of professional colleagues who were struck by his ideas and formed a nucleus of allies and disciples.

Today, the theory of the Oedipus complex has not been invalidated. But research in the psychology of children shows that it is not the boy's fear of his father that sends him on to the next stage of development. On the contrary, a frightening father may cause a boy—or a girl too, for that matter—to cling longer to the mother. Supporting and encouraging fathers, though, are known to help their children grow securely into successful adults.

DEVELOPMENTAL STAGES

Freud's insight that humans pass through developmental stages has been universally accepted, although these stages may now be designated in different terms. As a medical person, he started from the assumption that the human being is a biological entity whose psyche learns and functions by means of the body. What drives the spirit? What makes it go?

It was Freud's theory that the psyche is a system with a fixed amount of *erotic*, or sexual, energy which it invests in various ways. He called this energy *libido*, which means something like lust or zest for life. At each new stage, the individual's libido connects with a different zone of physical pleasure—a so-called *erotogenic zone*. This means that the psychological stages go hand in hand with biological development. At the same time, they are partly determined by the demands that the outside world makes on the growing child.

For various reasons, an individual's energies may become fixed at any one of these stages. Such a "fixation" prevents further development and creates neurotic conflicts when adult life brings new demands.

The first stage Freud designated is the *oral stage*, because a baby's first pleasure and experience of the world occurs mainly through the mouth. In this phase, the baby depends for comfort and survival entirely on others. In theory, people who fail to grow successfully out of this stage later remain dependent as adults. Their satisfactions are still focused mainly on oral activities and they absorb pleasure passively.

The next important phase a child must pass through is toilet-training. Freud called this the *anal stage*. It is likely to be a time of power struggles between child and parent. As children learn to "hold back" or "let go" of their feces, they gain a sense of control and independence. They experience pleasurable anal sensations and often they take quite a bit of pride and pleasure in their bowel movements. In Freudian terms, people whose development remains arrested in anal eroticism may turn out to be either very messy or exaggeratedly neat. They may be tight with money, ungenerous in friendship, cruel, and dictatorial.

The third stage occurs at the age of about three, when the child becomes aware of the genital difference between the sexes and begins to notice adult sexuality. In fact, Freud even toyed with an idea that our prehistoric ancestors may have been creatures who reached their reproductive maturity in three years. This is known as the *Oedipal stage*, which was described earlier. With it come erotic desires for the parent of the opposite sex and murderous wishes to get rid of all rivals.

SUBLIMATION

After the Oedipal stage, a so-called *latency period* sets in, a period of dormancy and forgetting. This is probably the part of childhood that many people see as a paradise of innocence, free of disturbing sexuality. During latency the child's energies are diverted to new channels of learning, in preparation for every kind of creative work and cultural achievement. Freud's term for this diversion of erotic energy toward intellectual and spiritual goals was *sublimation*.

Latency lasts until puberty, which finally prepares the way for sexual, social, and intellectual maturity. Freud called this end phase the *genital stage*, and considered it a consolidation of all the previous stages.

Needless to say, these developmental stages are not to be taken as literally and rigidly fixed occurrences. Rather, they sketch out a convenient theoretical model. In reality, stages tend to overlap, run side by side, and leave their residue in the adult personality.

WOMAN AS SPHINX

In putting together his theory of stages to maturity, Freud felt sure of his ideas on the development of men, but not quite so sure about the development of women. Living, as he did, before a time when fathers as well as mothers nurture little babies, he assumed without question that the mother or wet nurse must be the first love object of every infant, both male and female.

Anna Freud, Sigmund Freud's daughter,
established a reputation in her own right
for her work with children and her
contributions to psychoanalytic theory.

But whereas the sexual love of males continues to be directed toward women for the rest of their lives, the sexual love of young females has to be redirected toward men. What makes a girl turn from her first love—her mother—toward her father and later to men in general? It seemed to Freud that it must be the discovery that both she and her mother are missing an essential body part, namely, the penis. According to Freud, *penis envy* turns the girl toward a man for completion, and makes her wish for a baby to compensate for what she lacks.

This theory is ingenious but controversial, like so much of Freud's thought. It can neither be proved nor disproved, and many experts on the psychology of women reject it.

Regarding Sigmund Freud's relationships with women, we know that he was fond of his mother and his wife, and worked in great harmony with his daughter Anna. Women patients made up a majority of his private practice. But he had old-fashioned, stereotyped ideas about women. "Nature has determined woman's destiny through beauty, charm, and sweetness," he wrote early in his career, and he agreed with the nineteenth-century notion that women are in many ways weaker, but spiritually nobler, than men. At the same time, though, he had several close, intellectual friendships with enterprising, assertive women whom he admired.

Unconsciously, perhaps, Freud never stopped regarding woman as the Sphinx of the Oedipus myth, a combination of mother, lion, and bird—a creature able to nurture, but powerful enough to destroy as well as to soar above the earth.

At any rate, his good friend and supporter, the Princess Marie Bonaparte, reports that he once confided to her, "The great question that has never been answered and which I have not yet been able to answer despite my thirty years of research into the feminine soul, is 'what does a woman want?' "

And so it seems that the great analyst of the human psyche never quite solved the riddle of the Sphinx to his complete satisfaction, after all.

THE MIDDLE YEARS

Freud's quick ear and eye had a way of catching the unconscious at work, even in common, everyday situations. His mature writing extended the scope of psychoanalysis far beyond the doctor's office. He had begun to see that the difference between "abnormal" and "normal" emotions was often only a matter of intensity and degree. From observing sick individuals he took to observing the world, even the customs and beliefs of entire societies. He also revised his views on the human personality, sketching out an overall structure that is still fundamental to modern psychoanalysis.

ACCIDENTS AND THEIR PURPOSE

If you happen to lose your wallet, break a glass, or forget an appointment with the dentist, you may shrug it off as a mere accident. But according to Freud, all bungled actions of this kind have their psychological significance. Just as there are no indifferent dreams, there are no indifferent mistakes. In his book *The Psychopathology of Everyday Life* (1904), Freud analyzes the unconscious factors that are responsible for errors, forgetting, slips of the tongue, breakage, and every other kind of faulty performance, including accidental self-injury.

Take, for instance, the story of the psychiatrist who declared a patient "durable," when he meant to say "curable." Evidently he expected the cure to require a lengthy treatment and was looking forward to the steady income it would bring.

Or consider the case of the man who was reluctant to accompany his wife to a formal reception. To get ready, he opened the trunk in which he kept his dress suit, but before dressing he decided he needed a shave. When he came back, he realized that he had clamped down the trunk lid on the automatic lock. He searched everywhere for the key but couldn't find it. Since it was Sunday and no locksmith was available, the couple had to miss the reception. On Monday, when the locksmith opened the trunk, the key was found—inside. The husband was totally unaware of having placed it there and locked it up. Confronted with his apparently accidental behavior, he sheepishly had to admit that it got him his wish.

Not all unconscious intentions are so transparent. When it comes to losing an object, for example, many possible motives may be at work. Suppose you lost a scarf that was a gift from a friend. One reason might be that you think scarves are hot and scratchy, or that you think the color doesn't suit you. On the other hand, you might like the scarf but unconsciously resent the friend who gave it to you. It is also possible that the scarf represents some memory you would rather forget. Or perhaps, although your friend took pains to buy you the scarf you forgot to invite him to your Christmas party, and so you feel you don't deserve his gift. Finally, losing an object may be a sort of sacrifice to fate in exchange for some favor you hope to get. Losing the scarf might be like saying, "I'll give up my friend's present, if only fate will always let me keep my friend."

BODY LANGUAGE AND JOKES

It was Freud who first noticed that people's gestures often express unconscious impulses. In *The Psychopathology of Everyday Life*, he notes how a woman who was considering leaving her husband for another man toyed with her wedding ring, turning it back and forth, pulling it off, and putting it on again. He also describes how young girls, who were forced to wear their beautiful hair severely pinned up in those days, had a way of moving their heads so that the pins came loose and the hair cascaded over their shoulders at just the right dramatic moment.

Because *The Psychopathology of Everyday Life* pointed out things we all do—not just patients suffering from neuroses—it helped make the name of Sigmund Freud an international household word.

Freud, who was very fond of wit and humor, also wrote a book called *Jokes and Their Relation to the Unconscious* (1905). He thought that jokes, like dreams, give pleasure by a discharge of tension. Like dreams, jokes allow people to express impulses that they must ordinarily keep under wraps, such as aggression and hostility. Just think of the laughter released in a movie or at the circus when an ornate cream pie lands in some unlucky person's face. Other repressed topics that are given free rein in jokes are racism, religious prejudice, excretion, and sex.

THOUGHTS ABOUT HUMANITY

Freud wrote several important books about the nature and beliefs of humanity. In each he pointed out comparisons between individual neurotic behavior and the customs of entire cultures. In *Totem and Taboo* (1913), he aimed to show that the Oedipus complex is common to all people and that it has dictated some of the basic laws in tribal cultures as well as in Western civilization.

In *The Future of an Illusion* (1927), Freud wrote about religion. In his view, people develop religions to counteract the helplessness and anxiety that are fundamental to the human condition. Religion permits us to have our wish to stay permanently in the secure state of childhood. He points out that God is usually imagined as a father who makes the rules. Like children in a family, people who obey the rules are rewarded, whereas those who disobey are punished.

Finally, in *Civilization and Its Discontents* (1930), Freud came to the conclusion that civilized living requires many sacrifices from people. For the sake of peaceful coexistence we have to repress our aggressive instincts. The many things we would like to do if only we didn't have to stick to the rules of civilized living give us a permanent sense of guilt. He wondered if some day civilization might be changed to make it more satisfying to human needs. But he ended by saying that there may be "certain difficulties in the very nature of culture which will not yield to any efforts at reform."

THE TOTAL PERSONALITY

Freud's early ideas about the human psyche left many things unexplained. Much as he tried to see things in terms of scientific cause and effect, Freud had to concede that a person is not just a biological clockwork but a complicated organism shaped by numerous forces.

In 1923 he published a very important book, *The Ego and the Id*, in which he revised his basic theory of the psychic system. He expanded it and placed more emphasis on the total personality centered around the "ego" or self.

Originally, the main Freudian distinction was between the conscious and the unconscious regions of the mind. He called the conscious aspect the *ego*, which is Latin for the "I" or the self. To the unconscious part he assigned the term the *id*, which roughly means the "it." Now, in his new work, he outlined a third region of the human psyche, the *superego*.

EGO, ID, AND SUPEREGO

In Freud's new three-part personality structure, the basic and most primitive component is the id. Driven by the libido or life-force, the id responds only to the pleasure principle and never stops seeking satisfaction. The id is in the service of self-preservation and represents human passions and aggressions.

The ego, on the other hand, deals with the external world and its practical demands. The ego enables us to reason, solve problems, test reality, and adjust our impulses to the demands of our conscience.

As for the superego, it represents our conscience and our ideals. Formed by the demands made on us by our parents and other authorities, it is the self we think we ought to be. The superego can lead us on to great achievements, but it is also the judge and jury we carry around inside us. When the superego isn't satisfied it punishes the ego, much as a parent punishes a child. We tend to say "I could kick myself!" when we believe we've done things badly. Kicking—in the form of anxiety and depression—is the job of the superego. In some cases the superego can be cruelly severe, even to the point of driving a person to suicide. The superego's activities may be partly conscious and partly unconscious.

In summing up, Freud wrote that the ego serves three masters and is threatened by three dangers: the outside world, the impulses of the id, and the severe judgment of the superego. Because of this, the chief aim in psychoanalytic treatment is to help a person make better compromises between these three aspects of his or her self, resulting in less anxiety, less inhibition of functioning, and more pleasure.

MOTHER AND CHILD

Freud's own relationship with his mother was so close and loving that he never imagined anything but perfect harmony in the early bond between mothers and children. One of his associates, Otto Rank (1884–1939), proposed, however, that all neuroses originate in the child's first separation from its mother in the traumatic experience of birth. For a long time, Freud shrugged off Rank's famous birth-trauma theory as an exaggeration. But later, when he thought deeply about the widespread problem of anxiety, Freud modified his position.

In revising his earlier ideas on anxiety, Freud now saw it as a danger signal given by the ego. One important cause of anxiety, he thought, springs from the threat of losing love and security. It repeats the trauma of a child's first separation from the mother at birth. If the experience of separation and loss is often repeated during the child's orally dependent, or nursing, stage, it may well become traumatic. In early childhood, further disruptions of the bond between child and parents may be added to establish a pattern of frequent anxiety.

In the process of growing up, we absorb—or internalize—the presence of mother, father, and other caring people into our selves. We also transfer—or project—the image of those who love us unto the world outside. This gives us confidence that the world regards us with kindness and appreciation. We become enterprising and ready to cope with life's ups and downs. But without this confidence, a sense of inadequacy may haunt us. When we're up against problems and crises, we may unconsciously repeat the childhood calamity of losing the nourishing, sustaining parental presence.

To avoid anxiety, an individual may keep away from threatening situations and repress threatening ideas and impulses. But this kind of safety exacts a high price. It prevents proper growth and unfolding of the personality and deprives the individual of enterprise and a sense of freedom. Thus, anxiety avoidance is at the core of neurosis.

Nowadays, the early bond between parent and child is known to be of primary importance. To give children a good start in life the newest techniques of delivery, infant care, and child raising are designed to minimize any disturbances in this basic relationship.

AGGRESSION

The results of the First World War made a deep and terrible impression on Freud. As a doctor, he witnessed frightful mutilations and emotional impairments in soldiers returning from the battlefield. The pleasure principle seemed to him in no way applicable here, and he was forced to acknowledge the importance of destructiveness and aggression. In *Beyond the Pleasure Principle*, written at the end of the war, he proposed that the life instinct is offset in the psychic apparatus by a *death instinct*—an urge to destroy. In formulating the dual theory of psychic energy, composed of the sexual, or life, force and the aggressive, or death, force, he wrote, "I can no longer understand how we could have overlooked the universality of nonerotic aggression and destruction, and could have omitted to give it its true significance in our interpretation of life."

Freud's early ideas had the beauty of great simplicity. Over the years, his work became more complex and wider in scope, less influenced by biology, and more humane. Once his name was established, people traveled to see him and wrote to him from all over the world—letters that he answered in his own hand. What these people sensed in him was his earnest interest, his empathy (the ability to put himself in their place), and his generous desire to help them.

7

THE WORLD AS
HIS PATIENT

In the fall of 1902, Freud sent postcards to four Viennese colleagues, inviting them to get together in his study to talk about their work. This little Wednesday evening circle eventually grew into the famous Vienna Psychoanalytic Society, the first of many others that were later formed in major cities everywhere. Looking back over his life's work, Freud once reflected that the whole world had been his patient. Not only had he extended psychoanalytic theory to human existence in general, but his ideas and methods had been carried abroad like fertile seeds, by his students, patients, associates, and supporters.

AN INTERNATIONAL
MOVEMENT

By 1909, Freud's fame had reached America. He was invited to lecture at Clark University in Massachusetts. Accompanying him were two close associates, the Swiss psychiatrist Carl Gustav Jung (1875–1961) and the Hungarian, Sándor Ferenczi (1873–1933).

The following year, these three men, helped by supporters from all over Europe, founded the International Psychoanalytic Association. Later, it developed into a network of branch societies and

Group photograph taken in 1908 at
Clark University in Worcester, Massachusetts.
Standing, left to right: A. A. Brill,
Ernest Jones, and Sándor Ferenczi.
Sitting, left to right, are Sigmund Freud,
G. Stanley Hall, and Carl Jung.

training institutes connecting Europe and America. The association began holding its yearly international meetings, issued a periodical journal, and opened a publishing house to which Freud donated all the proceeds from his books.

CRITICISM AND DISSENT

No sooner was the International Association well established than several key members decided to break with the basic Freudian assumptions and move off on their own. Two of the most important dissenters were Alfred Adler (1870–1937) and Carl Gustav Jung. Both men disagreed with Freud's emphasis on the sexual drive in human development and in the formation of neuroses.

Alfred Adler believed that the basic human drive was not sexuality but aggression. Neurotic behavior was motivated by feelings of helplessness and inferiority. Freud himself later acknowledged the important role of aggression in the psyche, but unlike Adler, he didn't see it as the chief basis of personality formation. Alfred Adler later came to the United States, where he practiced and built up a following of his own.

Carl Jung's disagreement with Freud also centered on the idea of the sexual origins of neurosis. Jung began by playing down the role of sexuality and ended by abandoning it altogether. Instead, he turned to a spiritual and mythological emphasis that was hailed by his followers as "a return to a saner view of life." Freud's bitter comment was that "anyone who promises mankind liberation from the hardship of sex will be hailed as a hero, let him talk whatever nonsense he chooses."

Jung's defection was a painful blow for Freud, both professionally and personally. The Swiss psychiatrist was an influence to be reckoned with and later became world famous in his own right. He and Freud had been friends and their falling out came at a time when other friendships, such as those with his former associates Breuer and Fliess, had already broken up.

On the other hand, brilliant new colleagues were constantly joining the ranks. By the time of the International Congress of 1922, the association counted 239 members. On this occasion, two remarkable young women, Melanie Klein (1882–1960) and Karen Horney (1885–1952), came to present papers. Melanie Klein was to become a renowned children's analyst in England. Karen Horney founded her own institute and clinic in New York, and wrote an influential book, *New Ways in Psychoanalysis* (1939), in which she rejects Freud's theory of the role played by penis envy in female development. At about this time, too, Freud's daughter Anna became an official of the Psychoanalytic Association. Anna later fled to England with her father, where she continued a long, distinguished career as a children's analyst.

THREE BLOWS
TO HUMANITY

Freud was both famous and infamous with the general public. His writings provoked outrage as well as enthusiasm, and were often misrepresented to exploit their sensational qualities. On one occasion a meeting at which he spoke was pronounced upsetting enough to be raided by the police. Some of his associates were ostracized and even lost their jobs. Although Freud found all this regrettable, he considered it inevitable. In the objections raised by the public he seemed to recognize the defensive arguments of his patients—part of the phenomenon he called the resistance to psychoanalytic interpretations. It was not only his theory of repressed sexuality that aroused people's anxiety. As he saw it, science had dealt humanity three great blows. The first—Copernicus's discovery that the sun doesn't turn around the earth—displaced us from the center of the universe. The second—Darwin's work on evolution—

Freud, in 1937, with his chow Jofi

removed us from a unique position in the animal world. And the third—Freud's discovery of the unconscious—confronted us with the unpleasant notion that we are not masters of our own minds. He conceded that it was hard for humanity to forgive these blows.

SOMBER TIMES

In some photographs of Sigmund Freud we see a gray-bearded man with a tired and severe expression. By the 1920s, he had become famous and psychoanalysis was turning into a dynamic cultural force. But privately, the horrors of the First World War, the loss of his savings in the general economic collapse, the difficulty of supporting a large family, and the deaths of a much loved daughter and a favorite grandson had begun to cast a shadow of sadness over Freud's cheerful and sociable temperament.

As if all this were not enough, in 1923 he was forced to undergo the first of many operations for cancer of the jaw. Radium treatment followed, leaving him in great pain and, for once, unable to work. Even at that time, when little was yet known about the harmful effects of tobacco, Freud's nonstop cigar smoking was suspected of being the cause of his cancer. Eventually, in a series of further operations, part of his right jaw and palate had to be removed and he was forced to wear a huge artificial device in his mouth. This prosthesis, which he called "the monster," made eating and speaking painfully difficult. The surgery also deafened his right ear—the one he was in the habit of turning toward his patients—so that from then on, his office couch had to be placed to the left of his chair. But in spite of all this, Freud went on writing, treating patients, and smoking cigars until his death.

EXILE

In May 1933, after Hitler came to power in Germany, Freud's books were publicly burned in a bonfire in Berlin. The Nazi regime had started its campaign to eradicate the Jewish population of Europe. Burning the works of Jewish scientists, artists, and writers was only the start. But in spite of all the harassment going on around him, Freud had, as yet, no inkling of his great personal danger. He was old and ill, had little money, and was unprepared for emigration. Besides, he was helping to support his four elderly sisters and couldn't imagine leaving them behind.

When the Germans invaded Austria, the Gestapo raided the Freud family's home. They looted his safe, took Anna away for questioning, and kept her late into the night. Her parents were left in fearful uncertainty, not knowing if she had been tortured or sent to a concentration camp.

Just in the nick of time, Ernest Jones (1879–1958), Freud's young English colleague who was to become his biographer, persuaded Freud to make a last-minute escape to England. It took an international array of high-placed supporters to accomplish the difficult feat of moving the frail old gentleman to safety, together with his immediate family and his personal physician. Even so, the Germans exacted a large sum of money for his release, confiscated his bank account, and burned his unpublished writings. His four sisters were forced to remain in Vienna, where they were incinerated in a crematorium five years later. By that time, though, their brother was no longer alive to grieve for them.

England gave the famous refugee a near-royal welcome. He was asked to sign the Charter Book of the Royal Society, where his name now appears with those of other renowned discoverers, including Isaac Newton and Charles Darwin. Installed in a house outside London and grateful for the view of a pretty garden, Freud still conducted four analytic sessions a day and went on writing. But a moment arrived when, as he wrote to his friend, the Princess Bonaparte, his life had become "a little island of pain floating on a sea of indifference."

Freud died in London on September 23, 1939, in his eighty-fourth year. His former homes in Vienna and London are now mu-

*Freud, with his daughter Anna,
arriving in Paris, France, in
June 1938, on his way to refuge in
England after escaping from the Nazis.
The figure on the far right is
William C. Bullitt, U.S.
ambassador to Great Britain.*

seums open to the public. Among the things one can see there are his analytic couch with its well-worn Persian rug, and his collection of ancient Egyptian figurines. Most of his unpublished manuscripts, letters, and documents have been transferred to the Library of Congress in Washington, D.C.

AN AGE OF PSYCHOTHERAPY

Society has changed greatly since Freud's time, and so have some of the emotional problems we all face. For one thing, ideas about what is masculine and feminine behavior are no longer quite the same, and new disorders such as drug abuse now plague us like an epidemic. Sex is discussed a little more openly, and young people have a great deal more sexual freedom. Even so, the basic psychological symptoms and personality quirks are still with us. Today, we are more likely to recognize what a handicap these can be and we are more likely to try to do something about them. People tend to seek help for their anxieties, depression, pains, fears, and disabilities. A large establishment of psychiatrists, psychologists, psychoanalysts, counselors, and social workers now offers professional help. Psychological testing and counseling now often begin with young parents and small children and continue all through school, because it is hoped that early treatment can prevent problems from developing later in life.

PSYCHOANALYSIS TODAY

The particular specialty called psychoanalysis is practiced today very much the way the old master practiced it himself. Over the

past half-century, many of Freud's basic ideas have been absorbed into the mainstream of psychology. He is now generally considered to have been a genius well ahead of his time, whose hunches led him to more than one major breakthrough. As historian Peter Gay commented in the recent television documentary, "Freud Under Analysis"—"we live in a Freudian world. It is quite unthinkable to envision the world today without Freud's language and ideas" ("Nova," WNET Channel 13, February 17, 1987).

On the other hand, Freud has plenty of opponents and critics. What follows is a rough outline of what they have to say.

First, Freud is often thought to have placed too much emphasis on biology, especially on the sexual drive, as the main influence in personality development. Next, his methods are considered unscientific because he learned from observing his patients, his family, his friends, and himself, but made no systematic studies with controlled data. Finally, critics object that he took a mechanical view of the influence of the past on an individual's fate. This seems to play down the role that hope, effort, and free will can play in forming a strong, successful personality in spite of troubles early in life.

Even at the height of its fame the classical psychoanalytic treatment never served a very large population. People who want fairly quick results are not attracted by the slow and thorough way psychoanalysis works, nor by the way it delves into past history to examine the origins of the problem. Freudian analysis is a long-term, expensive commitment in which patients meet their doctors up to five times weekly for several years.

One test used to plumb our hidden thoughts is the Rorschach test whereby the person being tested interprets inkblot designs in ways that reveal psychological factors.

Doctors who practice psychoanalysis go through a long, difficult training. Analysts must have medical degrees before they can enter a psychoanalytic training institute that is part of the International or American Psychoanalytic Association. Here, they conduct treatments under supervision. At the same time they have to go through a training analysis of their own with a senior doctor.

NEW SCHOOLS
OF THERAPY

In general, though, psychological treatment was surely an idea whose time had come. In the wake of the Freudian school, numerous other schools of psychotherapy have sprung up, most of them inspired to some extent by the original talking cure. According to a recent "MacNeil/Lehrer News Hour" report, an estimated 80 million Americans living today are going to seek psychological counseling at some point in their lives, and some 250 different varieties of therapy ure available to serve them.

Nowadays, therapy is not necessarily practiced by a psychiatrist or psychologist. Social workers, counselors, psychiatric nurses, and members of the clergy have joined the field. Nor does psychotherapy necessarily mean meeting on a one-to-one basis. Group encounters and family therapy are now common. In some kinds of treatment talking may be combined with other activities, such as exercise, music, painting, or dramatic acting. And severely disturbed patients are now often treated by combinations of psychotherapy and medication such as tranquilizers and antidepressants.

THE MAINSTREAM
APPROACHES

Among the many types of therapy that are now practiced, two methods stand out in addition to psychoanalysis. The earlier of these is *behavior therapy*. The other, more recent, addition is *humanistic* or *client-centered psychology*, whose followers like to think of it as the "Third Force" among the therapies.

The roots of behavior therapy go back to behaviorism, the school of thought that believes that a genuinely scientific psychology must be based on observable fact and not on the patient's consciousness or feelings. The treatment method is based on the work of the American psychologist B. F. Skinner (b. 1904) and his findings about the ways animals discover and learn things.

Behavior therapists assume that most actions (or behavior) are basically learned and can also be unlearned and changed. Their aim is to modify certain undesirable behavior patterns by various techniques. On the whole, as in animal training, the system is founded mainly on rewarding behavior that is considered positive and discouraging that which is considered undesirable. Behavior modification does not explore the patient's feelings or past history. Instead, it sets simple, well-defined goals. This makes it particularly useful for people who want to be relieved of a definite, isolated symptom, such as alcohol dependence, cigarette smoking, or overeating.

The third mainstream approach—humanistic or client-centered psychology—was founded in the 1960s by Dr. Carl Rogers (1902–1987). In client-centered psychology, patients are called clients to indicate that they are in equal partnership with the therapist. Client-centered therapy is based neither on analyzing nor on retraining people. Instead, it is permissive and encouraging. According to Rogers, people have inborn tendencies toward health. The therapist's job is merely to help remove whatever obstacles are blocking the client's growth toward maturity and self-cure. The typical Rogers treatment is short, with more time spent discussing the present situation than the distant past.

The client-centered approach lends itself well to working with people in groups. It has led to the kind of group encounter movement in which people are brought together to discuss a common problem or to understand each other better. It has also become popular with

*A person acting out his fears in
a therapy session. At left is his therapist.*

A desensitization session in which the subjects stretch out, keep quiet, and relax. Desensitization means making a person less adverse to certain unpleasant stimuli, and may serve as a prelude to other forms of behavior therapy.

corporations and government organizations for training managers and executives.

Behaviorism and humanistic psychology are countermovements rather than heirs to Freud. But although these three approaches to the human mind would appear to be irreconcilable, in actual practice some therapists may combine methods and techniques to give patients the help they need.

HOW SUCCESSFUL IS PSYCHOTHERAPY?

The knowledge that psychological treatment enables people to live freer, happier, and more enterprising lives comes from observation and experience. Researchers are constantly devising new experiments to discover how, why, and to what extent psychotherapy is effective. But still these questions have a way of eluding proper scientific tests and measurements. Human beings and their emotional problems are so multifarious that it hasn't been possible to determine which treatment works best. As you can imagine, success very much depends on the situation of the patient as well as on the background, training, and skill of the therapist. On the whole, research has established that people who seek out treatment get better, provided they make a true commitment to it, and provided they see the therapist as sympathetic and accepting.

LOOKING AHEAD

From which direction can we expect to get fresh insights into the human mind and soul? A revolution in knowledge about the brain has been going on since the 1960s, and many experts believe that we are on the brink of discovering how the mind works in terms of chemistry and physics. New tools and techniques enable scientists to investigate the cells of nerve tissue on the molecular, or most basic, level. Neuroscientists can now analyze the brain's neurotransmitters, the chemicals that nerve cells release in order to communicate with other nerve cells. At the same time, molecular biologists are beginning to sort out the hereditary genes that govern certain developments in the nerves and brain. As for chemical drugs that can alter people's moods, temporarily calming them down or cheering them up, these have been a standard part of psychiatric medicine for the last thirty years.

When Sigmund Freud labored over his "neurology for psychologists" back in the 1890s, he could not even have dreamed of the knowledge and instruments that are available to researchers today. If Freud were alive now, he would surely be an enthusiastic participant in the adventures of modern neuroscience. No doubt he would also be fascinated by the parallels between brain functioning and the information processing done by computers.

Eventually, perhaps, neuroscience will be heading toward the goal Freud set for himself in his *Project for a Scientific Psychology*—the discovery of a universal theory of the mind. But this great synthesis of the psychological and physical sciences still lies very far ahead of us in time.

A GLOSSARY
OF TERMS

Anal stage. The developmental stage when children learn to hold back or let go of their bowel movements, thus gaining a sense of control and independence.

Behavior modification. Any treatment approach whose direct aim is to change a patient's behavior patterns by some sort of learning technique.

Client-centered therapy. One of the main approaches to therapy and counseling. Based on the belief that the patient (here called the client) has inborn powers of self-understanding and recovery.

Countertransference. The analyst's repressed feelings toward the patient. The analyst must be aware of the countertransference so as to maintain an objective attitude in the analytic relationship.

Death instinct. Freud's war experiences led him to believe that the pleasure principle was offset by another basic principle—an impulse for aggression, destruction, self-destruction, and death.

Defense mechanisms. Devices people use for keeping repressed ideas from becoming conscious. They serve to protect the individual from anxiety, guilt, and unacceptable impulses.

Ego. In Freud's three-part personality structure, the aspect of self that enables us to perceive the external world in accordance with the demands of reality.

Erotic. Having to do with sexual desire. The word comes from Eros, the ancient Greek god of love.

Erotogenic zones. Areas of physical pleasure such as the mouth and the genitals. During human development the libido connects with each of these zones in turn.

Free association. The basic technique used in the psychoanalytic session, in which the patient puts into words whatever comes to his or her mind.

Genital stage. The stage in development in which the individual has transcended the oral and anal stages and has reached physical and emotional maturity.

Hypnosis. A trancelike state, usually induced by a hypnotist. Under hypnosis, people become responsive to the hypnotist's influence.

Hysteria. A disorder that expresses itself in many different ways. Frequently the patient unconsciously transforms repressed anxiety into physical symptoms such as paralysis, blindness, pain or loss of sensations.

Id. From the Latin, meaning "it." The most primitive component of Freud's three-part personality structure, the id is made up of the instinctual drives that supply the psyche with its basic energy.

Latency. A period in child development when sexuality is dormant. In latency, energies are diverted to learning and intellectual creativity.

Libido. Freud's concept of the basic energy flow that fuels the life-force. At first, Freud thought of the life-force as mainly sexual. Later he broadened the idea to include love and pleasure, and finally he included a death instinct.

Neurology. The branch of medicine that specializes in the nervous system, both in its normal and its diseased states.

Neurosis. An emotional disorder characterized by a high level of anxiety and other distressing symptoms such as unreasonable fears, obsessive thoughts, compulsive action, or causeless depression.

Oedipus complex. Central to Freud's theory of human development. Based on parallels to the myth of Oedipus, it refers to the son's erotic love for his mother and corresponding rivalry with his father. The term *Electra complex* applies to a daughter's love for her father and rivalry with her mother.

Oral stage. The stage of infantile development in which pleasure occurs chiefly through the mouth.

Penis envy. According to Freud, a stage in the development of females in which they wish for a genital organ like that of males.

Phobia. An obsessive fear or anxiety without basis in reality.

Pleasure principle. The psychic force that makes us seek immediate gratification of impulses such as hunger or sex. It dominates the early life of children but is gradually modified by the reality principle.

Psyche. Another term for the mind, the spirit, and the self. The psyche is made up of Freud's three personality components, the id, the ego, and the superego, as well as the conscious and unconscious parts of the mind.

Reality principle. The principle that helps us control our impulses in keeping with the demands of reality, thus enabling us to deal with the problems of life.

Repression. A basic defense mechanism that consists of pushing painful thoughts and experiences into the unconscious part of the mind.

Seduction theory. Freud's early idea that many neuroses result from repressed childhood memories of one's having been sexually seduced or molested by an adult.

Sibling rivalry. Competition between the children (siblings) within a family, for the love and attention of the parents.

Sublimation. The diversion of erotic energies to intellectual and imaginative creativity.

Superego. In Freud's three-part personality structure, the aspect that represents our standards of conscience and our ideals.

Transference. A stage in psychoanalysis in which patients transfer to the person of the analyst feelings and wishes formed toward important people in their childhood. The process is necessary for successful analysis because it helps repressed emotions to surface.

Unconscious. The unconscious is the region of the psyche that is not directly accessible to awareness but that is nevertheless responsible for part of an individual's feelings and behavior.

Working through. The analytic patient's repeated confrontation with repressed memories and feelings. The process helps the patient resolve conflicts and reach for more constructive reactions.

RECOMMENDED READING

Fisher, Seymour, and Roger P. Greenberg. *The Scientific Credibility of Freud's Theories and Therapy.* New York: Basic Books, 1977.

Freud, Ernst, Lucie Freud, and Ilse Grubrich-Simitis. *Sigmund Freud: His Life in Pictures and Words.* New York: Harcourt Brace, 1976.

Freud, Sigmund. *The Standard Edition of the Complete Psychological Works of Sigmund Freud.* London: Hogarth Press, 1959.

Jones, Ernest. *The Life and Work of Sigmund Freud.* Edited and Abridged by Lionel Trilling and Steven Marcus. New York: Basic Books, 1961.

INDEX